Steve Miller

Spiraling Inward

The Rose Art Museum, Brandeis University

essays by Michael Rush and Mark Auslander
interview by Marvin Heiferman

Steve Miller: Spiraling Inward

The Rose Art Museum, Brandeis University
September 25, 2007 – December 16, 2007

Curated by Michael Rush

Design
Steve Miller & John Wilton
Editor
Michael Rush
Copy Editor
Gerald Zeigerman
Printer
Capital Offset Company, Inc., Concord, NH

ISBN 978-0-9761593-6-0

Library of Congress Control
Number: 2007935762

The Rose Art Museum
Brandeis University
MS 069, 415 South Street
Waltham, MA 02454-9110
t. 781-736-3434, f. 781-736-3439
www.brandeis.edu/rose/

The Rose Art Museum is sponsored by The
Rose Board of Overseers; by a grant from
the Massachusetts Cultural Council, a state
agency; and by The Rose membership
program.

Director's Foreword

An inevitable, if uneasy, alliance between art and science has existed for centuries. When confronted with an empty canvas or a blank blackboard, the artist and the scientist are one: both are poised to solve a problem that they have set for themselves. The most daring move the artist or scientist makes is that first gesture, that irreversible leap into the unknown of their own creativity. Before the erasures, wrong turns, frustrations, even hopelessness, there is that initial impulse that propels them toward a solution. Steve Miller is a pioneer in the contemporary arena of technology and art. His fascination with technology came from a desire to understand culture as an artist. From realist painter to installation artist, to "genetic portraitist," to abstract painter, Miller's impulse has been the same: to wrestle with the fundamentals of life through visual media.

Miller's work occupies the entire entrance floor of The Rose, and it is Steve whom I primarily wish to thank; he's been a joy to work with. I'm grateful to Mark Auslander, professor in the anthropology department and catalogue essayist, and to Marvin Heiferman who brought his depth of experience in art and technology to his interview with Steve Miller. Thanks as well go to Steve's associate John Wilton, who codesigned the catalogue, and to Gerald Zeigerman, our ever-ready copy editor.

I also want to acknowledge our extraordinary staff, several members of which are new, for their remarkable contribution to the exhibition. First, though, my thanks to someone who is not new, our assistant director for operations and exhibitions manager, Roy Dawes, who has overseen the installation, and his tireless crew: Janos Stone, Ryan Pressman, Jessica Hyatt, Natasha Bowdoin, Matthew Katz, and Matthew Robert Lane. Thanks also to our new registrar, Valerie Wright, who stepped in and organized all loan and shipping details; our department head, Tonja King, who was responsible for the daily logistics of the exhibition; and Stephanie Herold, our assistant director of development, who oversaw the collaterals and new efforts for members. Our graphic designer, Tony Morgan, contributed his customary superior work. Thanks also to our education director, Elizabeth Thach, for her inventive programming for all the current exhibitions, and assistant curator, Adelina Jedrzejczak, who serves many important functions at The Rose.

Finally, I want to offer special thanks to The Rose's Board of Overseers for their unflagging support of our programs. My gratitude, as well, to Brandeis president Jehuda Reinharz and provost Marty Krauss for their tremendous and steady support. I'm sure Steve Miller joins me in thanking Brandeis alum and Nobel laureate Rod MacKinnon for his profound inspiration.

—Michael Rush, *Henry and Lois Foster Director*

Steve Miller: Spiraling Inward

by Michael Rush

A painter in his studio sits before an empty canvas. The daily crucible of his artistic life is to answer a set of problems he has already posed for himself: where to begin; how to express with these materials the idea that burns inside his head; how to make his hands translate such feelings into meaningful shapes, colors, patterns, images?

The scientist in her lab sits before a microscope or faces a blackboard or a notebook with empty pages that await her drafts, hypotheses, guesses, or stabs at understanding the problems she has set for herself: how to uncrack the codes that will lead to the next step of understanding the mysteries presented, the basics of life?

All artists and scientists share this fundamental practice: the posing of problems and questions, the answers to which (the artwork, the discovery) become their life's pursuit.

For some artists, the impulses of art and science are one and the same. "Everything I do looks at the world through the lens of technology," Steve Miller says.[1] Like the painter Vija Celmins, who miraculously manages to translate the universe glimpsed in a night sky to the small frame of a canvas, Miller takes the invisible worlds of proteins and molecules and renders them palpable within the confines of a canvas, but a canvas that has been prepped not only with paint but, in any given work, with a digital photograph, a sonogram, an MRI, or a DNA code.

Miller's work at the borders of art and technology began with a certain discontent. "I had become disenchanted with painting," he says, "and began looking at the larger cultural context of which art was a small part. The larger part was mass media, financial networks, and the emergence of new technologies."[2] This was in 1980.[3] For his first solo gallery exhibition in New York, at White Columns, he created a multimedia computer installation he called *Network,* which analyzed financial commodities trading and the distribution of contemporary art. In the midst of a large, black-and-white-painted camouflage environment, he set up an electronic data screen on which it was possible for visitors to trade in the New York and Chicago commodities markets. Miller himself was a trader at that time, with his own small company. In one stroke, he had come a long way from painting.[4]

Such conceptual, interactive works were not to hold his attention for long. After building two more installations in the early 1980s (one for Artists' Space, which con-

*top: **Studio, lower Manhattan***
*bottom: **Brookhaven National Laboratory** Synchrotron Light Source*

tained live feed from the New York Stock Exchange, and another for the Bronx Museum, which mimicked a stereotypical "men's club trophy room," contrasting dramatically with the urban deterioration on the Grand Concourse just outside the museum at that time), Miller returned to the canvas with a vengeance, but armed now with the tools of the nascent digital revolution. He began to silk-screen computer-enhanced Rorschach blots onto canvas, as if wanting to "test" viewers' psychological states. He then used medical images as metaphors for cultural pathologies in paintings of damaged hearts and echocardiograms. Renditions of viruses and cancer cells started to appear in his paintings as well.

There are many precedents in the history of art for Miller's use of scientific tools and processes, particularly in the relatively recent art of photography. Photomicroscopy, a nineteenth-century invention that enabled the enlarging of miniscule views of objects under a microscope, was used by artists in the twentieth century to explore abstraction and the fundamentals of form. German artist Carl Strüwe's (1898–1988) photographs of single-cell algae—for instance, *Prototype of Individuality (Single Cells of Diatoms),* 1933—is especially relevant to Miller's work in its use of scientific tools to explore issues of identity and pure form. Dain Tasker, an American physician and amateur artist (1872–1964), used his professional access to radiography to create such visually haunting photographic works as *Lily—an X-ray,* 1930.[5]

László Moholy-Nagy (1895–1946), perhaps more than any other modernist, pioneered artistic uses of X-rays and other "tools," which he placed in the service of his profound interest in light. His cameraless "photograms" advanced the links between art, nature, and photography in ways that Miller capitalizes upon. Miller, however, despite his steady dances with new technologies, reveals himself fundamentally as a painter. Surely he has inherited expanded uses of photography from Moholy-Nagy, Karl Blossfeldt (1865–1932), and a host of others, but his trajectory stems more from Pollock, de Kooning, Warhol, and Rauschenberg than from Man Ray and Moholy-Nagy.

Miller's silk-screening techniques are essentially those of Warhol and Rauschenberg. In 1986, he began working with Robert Bardin and Donald Sheridan, both of whom worked for Rupert Smith, who ran Warhol's printing operations. Miller brought painted canvases to their printing studio, in Williamsburg, and the first images they screened were Rorschach blots that Miller had manipulated on a computer and then put into a silk screen.

Warhol's silk screens, in time, of course, radically altered this form of reproducible art-making, legitimizing it and making it very appealing to dealers and collectors. Of particular relevance to Miller's work are Warhol's *Heart,* ca. 1979, a "screenprint," as

he called them, of a heart apparently taken directly from a textbook, and *Philip's Skull (CAT Scan)*, ca. 1983, a print with deep blues and a thin, black tracing of a ghostly head.[6] Beyond techniques, however, Miller reflects Warhol's and Rauschenberg's affections for popular culture and social engagement. Arthur Danto has rightly described Warhol's "political genius": "Warhol's political gift was his ability to make objective as art the defining images of American consciousness."[7] His "Death and Disaster" series (car crashes, race riots, electric chairs) displayed a deep sensitivity to the downside of the glamorous culture with which Warhol was so identified. So, too, images of hearts and CAT scans, presaging, perhaps, his own untimely death, suggested a sensitivity to the temporality and decay of life. The aging skin lurking within the colorful portraits of Liz and Jackie belied the superficiality many have wanted to associate with Warhol. Miller, like Warhol, treats popular culture (expressed through imaging machines that diagnosticians use to discern illness, and references to costly pharmaceuticals) with the complexity of a clinician well versed in the signs of decline.

Miller's early experiences as a filmmaker and his ongoing use of photography are

Studio, Long Island Becky Rosko and Steve Miller

important paths to understanding his affiliation with Warhol, as well as his total integration of multimedia techniques in the service of his ideas about human nature and the fundamentals of life. In his recent works on canvas, Miller is advancing painting and printmaking to their next logical position as a multimedia object, as dependent upon the inheritances of the moving and still image as upon the techniques of painting. Unlike the commonly understood notion of "Multimedia" being an artwork that combines different materials and multiple forms (video, installation) into a multipart presentation, Miller is making the canvas the locus of a multimedia practice, in which the components (digital photographs, silk screens, acrylic paint) serve as elements of a composition that, in the end, can only be described as a "painting."[8]

While there is no denying that Miller's fascination with advanced scientific-imaging techniques and knowledge of particle physics comprise the DNA, so to speak, of his work, he is fundamentally interested in the principles and history of art. Like Delacroix, whose intense study of scientific color theorists—for instance, Michel-Eugene Chevreul and J. F. L. Merimee—provided theoretical bases for his experiments with color[9] that resulted in dramatic narrative paintings (not visualizations of color theory), Miller's engagement with genetics or proteomics[10] is a means of aligning himself with the most current thinking on the fundamentals of existence, which is the "narrative" that most interests him. "Genetics and particle physics are asking *the* questions about the origins of life and the universe," Miller says.[11] His passion, however, is not to contribute to these scientific theories but to provide the aesthetic voice that allows emotional entrance into these mysterious workings through the equally potent power of art. For Miller, the internationally shared visual vocabulary of scientific imaging with the focus on essential life research was "irresistible from the viewpoint of an artist."[12]

In the first years of this century, Miller was introduced to Brandeis University alumnus Rod MacKinnon, of Rockefeller University, in New York. In December 2003, MacKinnon was awarded the Nobel Prize for his studies of the movement of charged ions across the membranes of proteins to cells. Miller was given unprecedented access to MacKinnon's notebooks, drawings, and, diagrams, which became the springboard for the artist's current body of work.

Rod MacKinnon   *right:* **Notebook page** Rod MacKinnon

$$\frac{\begin{array}{r}218\\23\end{array}}{299}$$

3000 | 120

$$\frac{10}{2000} \quad \frac{1}{200} = .005$$

1.055 For carbon TET
1.365 For Toluene, 20 Joules, hr.c

we need the following quantities:

K (Thermal cond) $= 5.9 \ \frac{\text{milliwats}}{cm \ {}^{o}K}$ water   mult by 0.86 For $\frac{cal}{hr \cdot cm \cdot {}^{o}K}$

BTU 5.1

C (spec heat cap) → water: 0.99857 at 23°C (cal/g·c)   carbon tet 31.7 $\frac{cal}{gm \ mole}$
4.18 Joules/g·c   decane 75 "

S (mass density)   water 1, others close

These mean per mole of subst

1 Joule = 0.2389 cal

$\frac{Joules}{(cm \cdot sec \cdot {}^{o}C)} (cm)({}^{o}C)$

$S = 4\pi K a \Delta T \rightarrow \frac{Joules}{sec}$

MW 142 decane

$\Delta T = \frac{S}{4\pi K a} = \frac{2 \times 10^{-13} \ Joules/sec}{(4\pi)(.005 \ \frac{Joules}{sec \cdot cm \cdot c})(10^{-8} \ cm)}$

50 N
0.5

also could say

$$\iiint \nabla \cdot \vec{J} \ dV =$$

$= \frac{2 \times 10^{-13} \ Joules/sec}{6 \times 10^{-10} \ \frac{Joules}{sec \cdot {}^{o}C}}$

methanol
MW $\overset{19.5}{\overset{c}{}} = C$

$$\iiint -\frac{2Da}{r^3} \Delta C \ dV =$$

$\cong .001 \ {}^{o}C$

$\begin{array}{c} H \ 3 \\ O \\ H \end{array} \begin{array}{c} 12 \\ 3 \\ 8 \\ 1 \end{array}$

$\frac{4}{5.9}$
$.86$
$\overline{354}$
472
$\overline{5.074}$

$\nabla \cdot \vec{J} = \frac{d}{dr} \frac{Da}{r^2} \Delta C$

$= \frac{2Da}{r^3} \Delta C \times \frac{4}{3}\pi r^3$

$\begin{array}{c}12\\5\end{array}$
$.060$

34

$= \frac{-2Da}{4r^3} \Delta C$

$= \frac{8\pi}{3} Da \Delta C$

$\infty \ 6 \times 10^{-10}$

⊛ Probably answer is something related to $C = \frac{dq}{dT}$

$= 4\pi K a \Delta T$

$\frac{cm^2}{sec} + cm \times \frac{moles}{cm^3}$

$\frac{K}{c S} \times$ Guess for heat: since $\frac{\partial C}{\partial t} = D \nabla^2 C$ $\frac{moles}{sec}$

units: gives stuff created = $4\pi Da (\Delta C)$

$4\pi \ K \ a \Delta T$ Probably $\frac{\partial u}{\partial t} = a^2 \nabla^2 u = \frac{K}{cS} \nabla^2 u$

$4\pi \left(\frac{cm^2}{sec}\right)(cm)$ gives   heat added $= 4\pi \frac{K}{cS} a (\Delta u)$

units: $\frac{cal}{} \cdot cm \cdot deg = \frac{cal}{}$ or $4\pi \ K \ \Delta T$

If "collision" is a proper word to describe the interactions of particles within the body, so, too, do Miller's canvases reflect a collision of forms, gestures, methods, and materials. The seeming chaos in his work actually serves to provide a generous support for the scientifically uninitiated, teeming as it does with what we imagine to be the spasms of movements within ourselves—the unseen and unreflected-upon mass of ingredients and their movements that result in our functioning bodies. *Hovercraft,* 2006, for instance, with clusters of proteins, crossed wires, spray paint, and maps (all of his work is a mixture of photography, collage, drawing, painting, silk-screening), brings a street sensibility to the complex science it explores. The spray paint intrudes on the pictorial surface as if to distract viewers from the inaccessibility of the unknown, thereby reducing our anxiety over our lack of understanding.

The soothing, if somewhat moody, blue dominating *Soap Opera, the Second Season,* 2006, is so aesthetically alluring that, even if we can't decipher the relationship of the bubble-shaped proteins to the rest of the field, we feel Miller is guiding us with color through the maps of the invisible world. The inscrutable layers of text (all from MacKinnon's notebooks) that form the ground of *Illuminated Serum,* 2007, are blurred by thin, black lines loosely drawn or brushed across the canvas. A large, black, biomorphic blob that tapers off at the bottom of the painting supports a dense cross-hatching of white lines both unfolding and folding in on themselves. These lines (a computer model for a protein) closely resemble the wire mesh of a Bertoia chair in Miller's studio, which he has often reproduced in his drawings. Surely Miller has studied the painterly obfuscations of Jasper Johns.

This same mesh pattern is used to great effect in *Liquid Wrap,* 2006. Silk-screened elements (proteins, helix patterns) float in a barren space, colliding with each other on the canvas and becoming trapped in a yellow web (the chair back again) of crevices and orifices. Here, too, Miller offers a palliative to the viewer, with the mesh a calming yellow spilling out of the center of this curving mass of twisted grids.

Miller may have wanted to challenge the hegemony of painting in his early career, but he embraces it now with the evident vigor of an abstract expressionist. *Puppet State,* 2007, looks as if Franz Kline had taken a sudden interest in molecular biology. Black paint drips and splashes on and around snippets of written equations, obscuring them all the more. Miller's signature mesh (here colored a variant of black so subdued that it reads like blue) emerges from the pitch blackness at the center of the canvas, adding more chaos to an already dark terrain. Miller's physical relationship to the canvas suggests not so much an homage to MacKinnon's opaque calculations but, more, a struggle with the elusiveness of the scientist's advanced mathematics.

Miller's most recent work is fierce in its painterliness. As he continues his riffs on the

Hovercraft 2006 25x22" graphite, dispersion, silk screen on canvas

above: **Soap Opera, the Second Season** 2005 51x40 dispersion, silk screen on canvas
right: **Illuminated Serum** 2007 81x50.5" dispersion, silk screen on canvas

above: **Protein #385** 2004 50x38" graphite, silk screen on paper
right: **Liquid Wrap** 2006 57x39.5" spray enamel, dispersion, silk screen on canvas

above: **Super Symmetric** 2004 25x19" dispersion, silk screen on canvas

left: **Puppet State** 2007 81x59.5" dispersion, silk screen on canvas

lives of proteins, his canvases have become more feverish with content and painterly interaction. Three works from 2007—*Definitely Tested* (pages 72–73), *If They Exist* (pages 62–63), and *The Chicken and the Egg Problem* (page 69)—are so jammed with content (text, images of microscopes, protein enlargements, mesh, and whatever else) and expressive swirls of acrylic racing across the surface that they are dizzying to view. It's as if Miller's own self-discovery as an artist has reached such a peak of exploration that he feels like he's racing with time to get it all out there, much like the scientist on the verge of finding a cure for a deadly disease. It can't happen soon enough.

The respite of color that Miller has offered in several of his paintings is glaringly absent in his latest work. Lurking within the enormous energy of these canvases, there is an evident premonition of darkness and decay (perhaps entropy) that was apparent in some mixed-media works on paper from the late 1990s and later, including *Super Symmetric,* 2004. This very *non*symmetric painting looks like a depiction of post-apocalyptic roadside refuse, with enlarged molecules in search of regeneration. The mesh here is blackened, charcoal, burnt, suspended at the far right of the painting. In *Blackboard Jungle,* 2005, a white cloudburst of proteins is illuminated against a dark, Turneresque sky filled with notes, equations, texts, and arrows.

Even earlier, in his 2000 New York gallery exhibition, entitled *Neomorts* (a science-fiction term for technically dead humans kept alive by artificial-breathing devices), Miller addressed issues commonly found in seventeenth-century Dutch *vanitas* paintings. Instead of decaying fruit and dead animals, he presented common objects (candles, clocks, vases) that he had run through X-rays or MRIs and silk-screened onto paper. The melancholic nature of these works reappears in such recent paintings as *Increasingly Implausible,* 2007 (page 71). Here, feelings of intimacy with the most essential life-forms of molecules and proteins is matched by a sense of disintegration, as dark blotches of paint spill recklessly beyond the edges of the canvas. Miller is warning us, or, at least, reminding us, of the temporariness of the biological. The race to understand life, exemplified in the swift, urgent jottings in MacKinnon's notebooks, is ultimately enmeshed with an endpoint: death, the black hole, revealed. The utter optimism at the base of MacKinnon's work is shadowed in Miller by gathering clouds and black drips.

Perhaps Warhol's journey, yet again, is instructive here. His extraordinary series of "Shadow" paintings from the late seventies (he described them as "disco-décor"[13]) reveal a prescient sense of death that was expressed full blown years later in his suite of silk-screened paintings based on da Vinci's *The Last Supper*. Warhol focuses on

Blackboard Jungle 2005 36x34" dispersion, silk screen on canvas

Jesus' forlorn face, encasing the downcast eyes in squares of yellow the color of bile and a mournful blue. For Warhol, as well as for Miller, silk-screening is the method that allows for the multiple layering of emotion and foreboding.

Although the intentional reproducibility of many of Warhol's silk screens may be thought to mimic the endless repetition of life after death, Miller eschews reproducibility. Each of his works is unique. In this way, he is respecting the irreducibly singular identity of his subject matter. Molecules may cluster by the millions in every organism; proteins, identical from person to person, may provide the engine of life; yet, in the mystery of it all, each organism is different. In his art, Miller asserts the individuality that defies mass culture and the biology that refuses, thus far, to relinquish its mortality.

Michael Rush is the Henry and Lois Foster Director of The Rose Art Museum. His widely translated books include New Media in Art *(1999, 2005) and* Video Art *(2003, 2007), both published by Thames and Hudson.*

Protein Model Rod Mackinnon's office, Rockefeller University

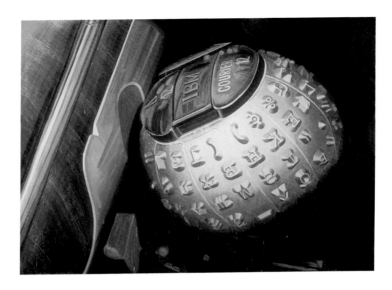

Daily Planet 1984 72x96" oil on canvas

1 Steve Miller, in an email communication with author, June 22, 2007.
2 Ibid.
3 In the late 1970s, Miller had also made short, abstract Super 8 films that were shown in several alternative festivals of the time, and also worked as an assistant director on commercial films in New York.
4 Despite his protestations, Miller's interest in painting has never waned. Well into the 1980s, his works on canvas approached photorealism, albeit with a techno twist. He painted prototypic, pre-digital imaging tools, such as an early newspaper printing machine (*Press,* 1983) and IBM's electric typewriter (*Daily Planet,* 1984).
5 For more on Dain Tasker and German artists who used photomicroscopy, see AnnThomas, *Modernist Photographs* (Ottawa, Ont.: National Gallery of Canada, 2007), 64, 172.
6 See Frayda Feldman and Jorg Schellmann, *Andy Warhol Prints, A Catalogue Raisonné 1962–1987,* 4th ed. (New York: Distributed Art Publishers, 2003), 236, 310.
7 Arthur Danto, "Warhol and the Politics of Prints," in Feldman and Schellmann, 13.
8 For an enlightening discussion of the interrelationship of cinema, visual art, the digital revolution, and contemporary notions of "representation," see Philip-Alain Michaud, *The Movement of Images,* exhibition catalogue (Paris: Centre Pompidou, 2006), 15ff.
9 See Nina Athanassoglou-Kallmyer, "Cézanne and Delacroix's Posthumous Reputation," *Art Bulletin* (March 2005), 118.
10 The study of the source code for life.
11 Steve Miller, in an email to the author, March 27, 2007.
12 Ibid.
13 See Feldman and Schellmann, *Andy Warhol Prints,* 29.

Protein #364 2004 40x30" graphite, silk screen on paper

Protein #356 2004 40x30" graphite, silk screen on paper

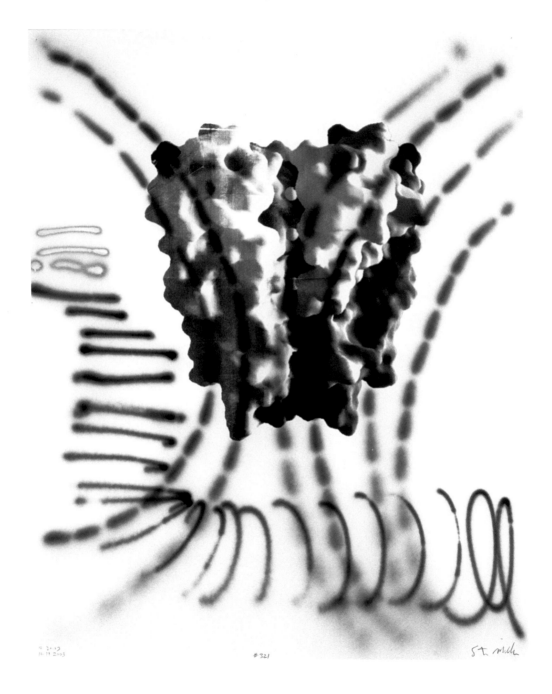

Protein #321 2003 50x38" spray enamel, silk screen on paper

Protein #203 2002 50x38" graphite, silk screen on paper

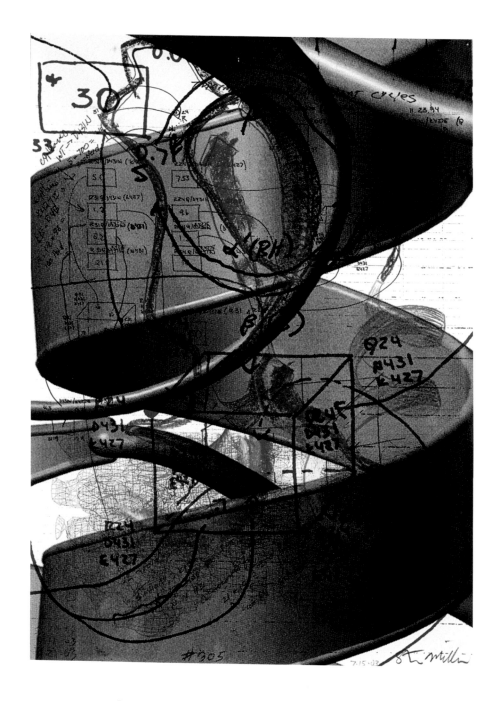

Protein #305 2003 19x13" inkjet, pencil, silk screen on paper

Protein #405 2005 19x13" graphite, silk screen on paper

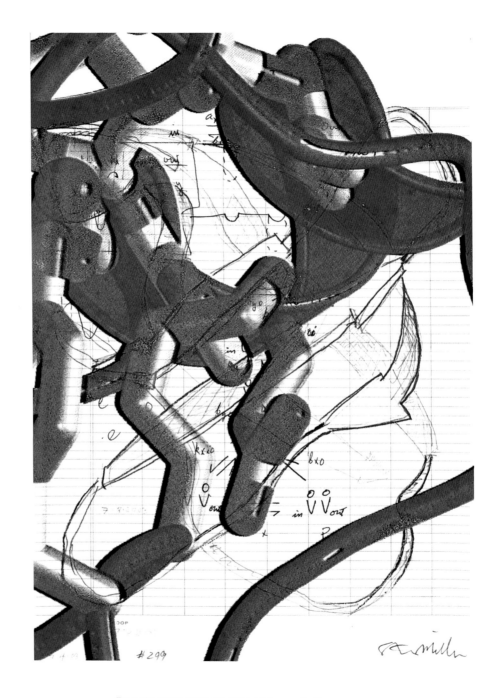

Protein #299 2003 19x13" inkjet, pencil, silk screen on paper

Protein #395 2004 19x13" pencil, enamel, silk screen on paper

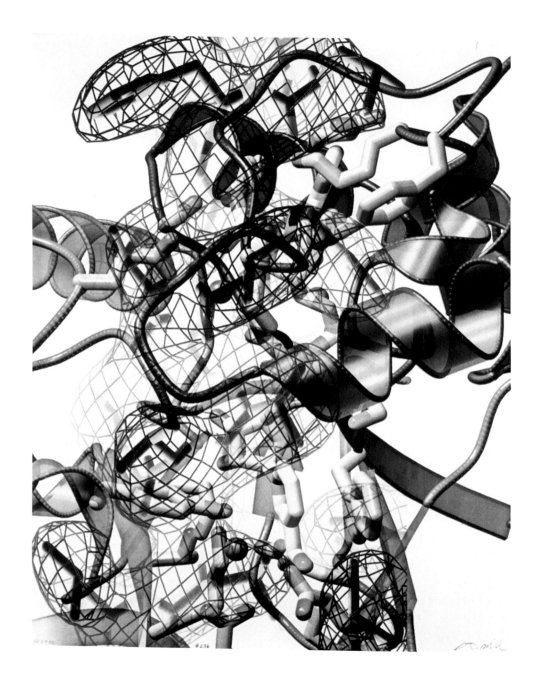

Protein #236 2002 50x38" silk screen on paper

Divination in the Age of DNA: (Re)reading the Entrails

Mark Auslander

For millennia, in a vast range of human cultures, ritual specialists have sought to illuminate hidden mysteries of the body and the universe through a diverse set of ceremonial practices. Processes of divination often address the basic existential questions of illness, affliction, and misfortune: Why me? Why now? Who's to blame? Among the most ancient of human practices, divination remains with us in advanced industrial societies, although often in forms that we may not consciously recognize.

Classic divinatory practices often proceed by symbolically dramatizing and transcending a core set of structural oppositions: revelation and concealment, visibility and opaqueness, surface and depth. Consider, for instance, the ancient practice of consulting the entrails of sacrificed eagles. The perceived usefulness of the eagle in divination is presumably related to the bird's far-seeing capacities. This potential for extraordinary externally directed vision is, in effect, bundled together with the diviner's inspection of the animal's most opaque and inaccessible elements—its intestines. The net symbolic effect is to promote extraordinary "vision" into the most hidden and enigmatic domains of existence. Indeed, our word "omen" is derived from the ancient Greek term *oinos,* the eagle or other high-flying birds of prey. Through intimate encounters with the opaque interior of celestial birds, we are afforded glimpses of the shadowy future here on earth.

These paradoxes are integral to augury. The stock-in-trade of the diviner is ambiguity and overlapping genres, complex plays of light and shadow, rapid movement and stillness, indirect glimpses and mirrored reflections, all as if to emphasize the woeful insufficiency of conventional vision and ways of knowing in the face of mystery. As they consult the most minute stretches of intestine, oracles often chant or recite in dense, esoteric language, promising to bring "clarity" and "certainty" even as their clients become increasingly uncertain of the meaning of the proceedings unfolding in front of them. As a great, winding road within the body, the intestines often serve as an apt metaphorical tableau of the intricate twists and turns of destiny; deciphering each knot, spot, swelling, blotch, patch, or lesion in their interior linings affords hints of the obstructions and challenges encountered by individuals and communities as time itself unfolds (Abbink 1993).

In large measure, our contemporary popular fascination with DNA and molecular biology recalls many of the archaic dynamics of divination. Genetic codes seem to promise us access to hitherto inaccessible mysteries, serving as enigmatic mirrors into our innermost selfhoods; we seem suspended between faith in the certainties of science and a longing to transcend the conventional protocols of rationalist modernity (Palmie 2007). Steve Miller's work hovers on this cusp, engaged with cutting-edge scientific work while summoning up the ancient aesthetic repertoires of the diviner. The images in his Protein series are never confined to a single visual style; they necessarily shift back and forth among multiple aesthetic registers, as if to emphasize that the building blocks of life cannot be grasped by any single mode of representation. Solid shaded surfaces oscillate with grids that recall industrial design, elegantly sculpted curves coexist with roughly sketched lines, microscopic pitted asteroids glimpsed through an electron microscope are slashed through with notations that might be scribbled on a chalkboard. As we spiral inward seeking the spiraling structures of amino acid that underlie all life, we are necessarily exposed to multiple forms of vision and sensation. Like the intestines of consecrated sacrificial animals held up toward the light

by ancient augers, Miller's assemblages simultaneously move in celestial and earthly directions. His *Protein #352* is suspended between the ethereal (some molecules rising like balloons as if toward heaven) and the excremental (roughly sketched structures sagging into the depths).

The divinatory imagery that runs through Miller's work reflects, in part, the enormous amount of interpretive work required of molecular biologists as they "translate" the X-ray film that has captured crystallized proteins. The thousands of diffraction spots generated by a protein need to be painstakingly worked out, with reference to the number of electrons in the electron shell of each kind of constituent atom within the crystal. (This work is especially challenging in the case of membrane pro-

Protein #352 2004 40x30" graphite, spray enamel, silk screen on paper

teins, which have especially interested Miller, since the highly mobile nature of these proteins renders crystallization especially difficult.) The researcher must, in effect, superimpose many two-dimensional cross sections of the structure over one another to generate a three-dimensional model of the miniature crystallized topography (Pietzsch 2007). Not surprisingly, many of Miller's images contain renditions of two-dimensional patterns that meld into complex three-dimensional structures, superimposed over pages from the scientific notebooks of the Nobel Prize winner Rod MacKinnon. The resulting works call to mind the extraordinary notebooks of Leonardo da Vinci, in which science, art, mirrored writing, and mystical vision converge in a dizzying array of unexpected twists and turns.

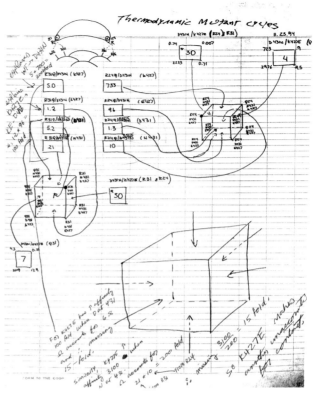

Writing and Revelation

For millennia, diviners have been fascinated by written words and symbols, sensing mystical attributes in the power of literate representations. (It is even possible that some of the world's writing systems emerged out of revelatory visions attained in altered states of consciousness.) In the late 1980s, I spent more than a year researching a movement of mass witch-finding as it swept across portions of south-central Africa. Spirit-possessed diviners wielding mirrors, which they compared to X-ray machines and TV cameras, claimed to be able to "read" the amount of witchcraft substance inside the body of each villager, who was forced to stand within a "circle of truth." Holding up the mirror, the oracle screeched out a long list of numbers and letters: "fifteen-stroke-eleven-stroke-twenty-seven!" These numbers of cuts would then be razored into the villager's chest, arms, and back. In effect, each person's body was transformed into a tangible text, through which his apprehended moral state was made legible to the entire community (Auslander 1992).

In a comparable fashion, Miller is drawn to the written words, numbers, and equations of Rod MacKinnon's scientific notebooks, which fill the spaces in and around his mysterious proteins. In *Blackboard Jungle,* 2005 (page 19), a cratered, white protein emerges out of the esoteric and frenetic equations scribbled in white chalk. In *Protein #202*, out of the background of a typed scientific paper the three-dimensional skeleton of a protein takes form. Here, we glimpse a new twist on the old idea of spontaneous generation, as intricate written equations seem to give birth to the very building blocks of life.

In numerous cultures, divinatory writing is rife with contradiction and paradox, and divinatory performances, ultimately a serious business, often occasion playful moments of hilarity and parody. Appropriately, the titles of Miller's works at times hilariously contrast with the images they reference; thus, *Crystal Clear,* 2007, refers to an enigmatic image of a power strip atop an impossibly cluttered surface (perhaps covered in ice crystals), while mysterious written notes are glimpsed below. The title seems to point to one of the central challenges in the study of membrane proteins, the great difficulty in transforming them into highly structured crystals so that they may be subjected to X-ray structural analysis. In turn, *Fear of Flying,* 2003, is the title of a painting of a meteorlike protein that seems to be rapidly propelled through space. In other works, humor is generated through text within the image itself. In *Crash*, 2006, crystalline structures are pressed against one another above the enigmatic words, "Be aware/Move the manipulator aside." The phrase evidently evokes the mechanical instruments used in laboratory work, as well as the biochemist who seeks to "manipulate" the fundamentals of life—by, for instance, crystallizing proteins in order to grasp how and why they fold themselves so perfectly in noncrystalline states. In Miller's witty *Protein #444* (page 39), a map of the genetic code is superimposed upon our other "code" for life: Martha Stewart's magazine *Living.*

Crystal Clear 2007 38.5x28" dispersion, silk screen on canvas

Crash 2006 26x20.5" dispersion, silk screen on canvas

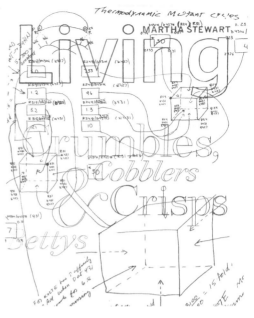

Protein #444 2005 50x38" pencil, silk screen on paper

The Dance of Life: Bodies and Machines

Throughout history, diviners and spiritual healers have probed the mysteries of the universe through bodily contortions, in dance and related forms of regulated, rhythmic movement. In subordinating the self to the complex patterns of the dance, the diviner offers body and soul to the greater structures of the universe that lie beyond our everyday perception. As many ritual specialists report, at a certain point you cease to dance the dance and the dance begins to dance you (Shore 1996). Within the intricate structures of dance and music, the seeker becomes attuned to the greater harmonies of existence. In concerted motion, our physical bodies, paradoxically, become windows to esoteric knowledge beyond flesh and beyond mere embodiment.

In a recent essay, Natasha Myers (2006) explores the ways in which X-ray crystallographers and molecular biologists in the laboratory contort their bodies and even grasp one another's hands and arms in order to illustrate and "feel" how proteins bind and reconfigure themselves in various biochemical operations. In so doing, Myers argues, researchers simultaneously assert, in a formal sense, mechanistic models for understanding proteins with mathematical precision, while evoking, in a phenomenological sense, imaginative dramas in which proteins are figured as living, intentional, and sentient beings.

A similar duality, hovering between the mechanistic and the animate, pervades Miller's images. In nearly every work, we are treated to mechanical structures—from lattice arrays and architectural elements to power strips and bottle openers—juxtaposed against evocations of human or animal bodies. At the bottom of *Protein #342,* 2003 (page 42), we see minimal abstract representations of molecules that congeal into a three-dimensional rendition of the larger protein structure, rendered in a form that recalls a clenched human fist. In *Hovercraft,* 2006, the title leads us to read the assemblage of spherical molecules as a mechanical mode of transportation skimming above the sketched-out surface below. Yet, the shadowy textures of this floating conglomerate feel like a living, pulsing body of some sort. *Protein #220,* 2002 (page 42), appears composed of mechanical components, centered on rounded shapes that

Potassium Channel
2007 80.5x81" dispersion, silk screen on canvas

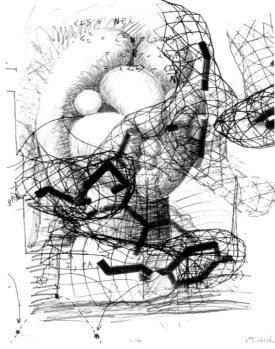

recall human eyes. In *Illuminated Serum,* 2007 (page 13), the metallic, monochromatic, and abstracted sheets of the double helix frame a throbbing, yellow mass that seems on the brink of active life.

Consider, as well, *Super Symmetric,* 2004 (page 17), presumably a reference to super-symmetric quantum field theory and allied forms of string theory. The image evokes an industrial wasteland of sharp lattices and rusting piping. Yet, through it runs a smooth tube (the fabled "string" of string theory?) that looks remarkably organic.

These virtual bodies themselves alternate among different levels of interiority and exteriority, evoking skeletal frames, solid musculature, nerve pathways, and

covering skin. Most important, these bodily images move in every possible way— they envelop, fold up, unfold, corkscrew, and reach out. They are, simultaneously, abstracted blueprints and vital breathing, palpitating organisms. The essence of detached scientific modeling, they are, at the same time, fundamentally present, tangible, and enlivened.

This necessary tension between modeling and organic vitality, between mathematical abstraction and embodied sensation, is brilliantly captured in *Potassium Channel,* 2007. The work plays on the obscure data of X-ray crystallography to afford us a remarkable image of the ion passageways that span cell membranes and regulate a great array of necessary organic functions (even the rhythmic contraction of the heart muscle relies on the regulated ebb and flow of potassium). Significantly, the 2003 Nobel Prize for Chemistry was awarded to Rod MacKinnon for, among other things, determining why larger potassium ions move across cell membranes while smaller sodium ions do not. (This research is also directly referenced in Miller's 2002 work *Protein #239*.) In *Potassium Channel,* we sense, almost kinesthetically, the diffusionary flows that make possible the survival and function of every cell in our body; the overlapping swaths of textured color dissolve into the abstracted forms of equations, which, presumably, represent the variations in charge density that account for the variations in membrane permeability. Sodium ions, with greater charge density, are associated with larger water shells, and become more bulky than potassium ions; thus, they are less likely to pass through the membrane channels, whose structure allows potassium to shed its surrounding water.

A similar juxtaposition between the abstract and the tangible presents itself in *We Need the Following Qualities,* 2007. At the top of the image, we read the scribbled phrase, "We need the following qualities," followed by thermal and related specifications in the abstract form of equations. Emerging out of the flat field of precisely articulated qualities is a large crisscrossing mass of taut tendons that hint at a pulsing, interior mystery.

Modeling and organism are humorously conflated in *Thought Balloon,* 2007. Abstracted representations of cellular building blocks and a latticework that seems to evoke a neural network are confined within a large, dark field that recalls the "thought balloons" of a cartoon strip. Yet, there's another joke here: Neurochemical elements within the brain are precisely what makes thought, and all abstracted models, possible in the first place.

Modeling and organic processes, as well as science and faith, are also coordinated in the sophisticated composition *Signal Relay,* 2003 (page 47). The title refers to the complex switchpoints through which interior processes within cells are coordinated across vast networks of cells in a given or-

Electrostatic Free Energy of Charge Transfer

Protein #239 2002 50x38" silk screen on paper

We Need the Following Qualities 2007 38.5x29" dispersion, silk screen on canvas

Thought Balloon 2007 25x20.5" dispersion, silk screen on canvas

ganism. In the lower foreground, we see a naturalistically rendered protein; above it extend more abstractly rendered curling strands bathed in light. These are in sharp contrast to the shaded and dark upper swaths of background, which appear to evoke the outer boundaries of the cell itself. Between the solid protein and the upper coiling strands is a powerful burst of energy that seems to evoke the very essence of vitality. For all the rigorous scientific modeling that informs this work, it is a profoundly spiritual piece, perhaps echoing Michelangelo's rendition of the touch of life between Adam and his Creator in the Sistine Chapel. As in the book of Genesis, in the face of cosmic darkness a voice proclaims, "Let there be light." Enlivened and illuminated, the bright, unfolding strands reach out into the void between cells toward their distant, invisible counterparts.

Romancing the Protein: Love Is All We Need

What precisely animates the proteins that dance across Miller's pages and canvases? In some instances, at least, the answer is *eros,* the impossible attraction and longing for the union of bodies and souls across chasms of distance and difference. Suggestively, *Ongoing Advances*, 2003 (page 49), presents a clever play on words; in addition to the steady progression of science, Miller hints at the colloquial sense of "advances" in a romantic or sexual sense. I read the sketchy, transparent figure to the left as male, propositioning (and exchanging energy with) the more solid molecular female form to the right. In many other works, contrasting forms reach out across empty space, strands and tentacles intertwining, co-penetrating and dissolving into one another. In *Ice Queen*, 2006 (page 51), a miraculous spiral at the core of our existence curves alluringly in all her cold, austere, and entrancing beauty. In the most intimate interstices of life, it would appear, the fundamentals still apply, as time goes by.

The Spaces in Between

This reminds me of a conversation I had in the late 1980s with a diviner in eastern Zambia, whom I shall call Elias. After a long talk with me about my life in America, Elias asked me, "What do you Americans actually see when you look at another person?" I responded, a little puzzled, that we just see the other person. "No," he said, "what do you see in between you and that other person?" I responded, even more confused, "Just empty air—that's all there is." Elias looked at me, sadly, with great compassion, and asked, "You don't see everything that binds you to that other person—the love, the hate, the longing, the fear? You don't see everything that fills the space between us and within us?"

Years later, pondering the art of Steve Miller, I might be able to give Elias a better

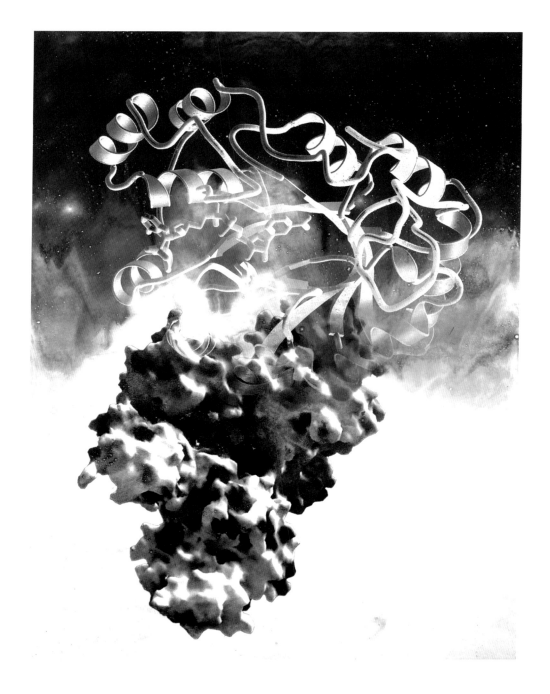

Signal Relay 2003 50x37.5" dispersion, silk screen on canvas

answer. In the intricate dances of his proteins, the elemental building blocks of life, we glimpse, as through a distant mirror, the full spectrum of human emotional registers, precisely what had seemed banished from the scientific world view since the seventeenth century. Like the animal entrails studied by ancient diviners, the layered surfaces of Steve Miller's art take us on travels into what most intimately surrounds us and sustains us at levels that are simultaneously material and immaterial, rationalist and spiritual. Through sensuous encounters with the very foundations of our flesh, we come to know what is emphatically beyond flesh, beyond direct corporeal sensation. Miller thus provides us with a privileged window into the paradoxical operations of scientific consciousness, which seeks to transcend the conventional circumstances of our bodily experience by generating models and metaphors that are inevitably derived from embodied, felt experience. In his remarkable corpus, Steve Miller reminds us that even when we most seek to leave the confines of our corporeal shells, we are, in the final analysis, fundamentally creatures of our bodies. Even in the seemingly invisible, empty spaces between us or between our constituent elements, we are bound to one another by earthly fear and longing, passion and love, despair and hope.

Mark Auslander is an assistant professor of anthropology at Brandeis University, where he directs the graduate program in Cultural Production. He has written on diverse topics, including mass witch-finding in Zambia, the cultural politics of HIV/AIDS art in South Africa, and the symbolism of race and memorial space in the American South.

References

Abbink, J. 1993. Reading the Entrails: Analysis of an African Divination Discourse. *Man,* new series, Vol. 28, No. 4 (December), 705–26.

Auslander, Mark. 1992. Open the Wombs. *Modernity and Its Malcontents: Ritual and Power in Africa.* Chicago: University of Chicago Press.

Myers, Natasha. 2006. Animating Mechanism: Animations and the Propagation of Affect in the Lively Arts of Protein Modeling. *Science Studies,* Vol. 19, No. 2, 6–30.

Palmie, Stephan. 2007. Genomics, Divination, "Racecraft." *American Ethnologist,* Vol. 34, No. 2, 205–22.

Pietzsch, Joachim. 2007. Protein Folding Technology. http://www.nature.com/horizon/proteinfolding/background/technology.html (Accessed 6/23/07).

Shore, Bradd. 1996. *Culture in Mind: Cognition, Culture, and the Problem of Meaning.* Oxford: Oxford University Press.

right: **Ongoing Advances** 2003 75x51.5" dispersion, silk screen on canvas

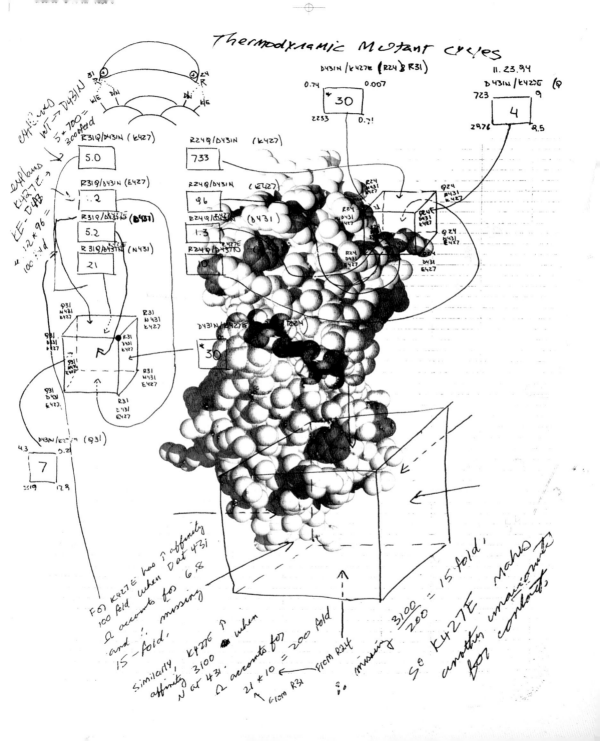

Thermodynamic Mutant Cycles

11.23.94

D43N / K427E (R24 & R31)

0.74		0.007
	30	
2233		0.71

D43N / K427E (R31)

723		9
	4	
2976		9.5

R31Q/D43N (K427)
5.0

R24Q/D43N (K427)
733

R31Q/D43N (E427)
.2

R24Q/D43N (E427)
96

R31Q/D433/5 (D431)
5.2

R24Q/D437N (D431)
1.3

R31Q/D43N (N431)
21

R24Q/D437N
10

D43N/K427E (R24)
30

D43N/K427E (R31)
7

4.3		5.21
2519		12.8

For K427E has ↑ affinity
100 fold when D at 431
Ω accounts for 6.8
and ∴ missing
15-fold.

Similarly, K427E ↑
affinity 3100 when
N at 431.
Ω accounts for
21 × 10 = 200 fold

missing 3100/200 = 15-fold!
So K427E makes
another unaccounted
for contact.

Silver Mine 2005 24x18" pencil, enamel, silk screen on canvas

Ice Queen 2006 24x18" pencil, dispersion, silk screen on canvas

Dr. Robert Sweet Group leader and biophysicist, Brookhaven National Laboratory

Every Body a Spectacle

An Interview with Steve Miller

Marvin Heiferman

Today, electronics and automations make mandatory that everybody adjust to the vast global environment as if it were his little home town. The artist is the only person who does not shrink from this challenge. He exults in the novelties of perception afforded by innovation. The pain that the ordinary person feels in perceiving the confusion is charged with thrills for the artist in the discovery of new boundaries and territories for the human spirit. He glories in the invention of new identities, corporate and private, that for the political and educational establishments, as for domestic life, bring anarchy and despair. — Marshall McLuhan, 1968[1]

> **Marvin Heiferman:** *This quote by Marshall McLuhan, which I find myself returning to often, seems to suggest some ways to start this conversation about your work. In the past, you and I have talked about artists' contributions to the visual language and their responses to the technology of their time. What is the visual language at work in your work?*

Steve Miller: Visual language today is complex; I don't think we can really say it is one thing or another. At first, I responded to McLuhan's claim, that artists are the only people who don't shrink from the challenge of facing up to novel perceptions, by saying, "Oh, yeah. Absolutely right." But now that I'm thinking about it—and about Google, YouTube, and MySpace—it seems like everyone today is more comfortable communicating with and through technology, which I think is the point of the exhibition, in a way. What used to be considered specialty languages no longer are.

People understand that information, image, and language systems can change and change quickly. Every artist I know uses Photoshop, and so does everyone else. Anyone can capture and manipulate images—adjust, annotate, and distribute their snapshots, animations, and home movies. Today, visual culture is much less specialized than when I started out.

> *When was that, and what kinds of ideas, images, and issues interested you then?*

In the early 1980s, I started to use computers to manipulate and translate images. I became increasingly interested in what happened when an image was reprocessed. Back then, you could put an image onto a computer and digitize it, have it automatically morph into another form of visual language, which seemed advanced at that time. You went to specialty studios and worked for hours on what can now be accomplished by pressing a single button on a home computer. But what was important to me was the notion that you could take an image, put it through a translation system, and automatically code it.

When you think back to that time, there were other artists who were also interested in taking images from culture and translating them, but perhaps in a more low-tech way. In the 1960s, pop artists repurposed and repainted imagery from mass culture. In the late 1970s and through the 1980s, another generation of artists began appropriating images—this time by rephotographing them, using another kind of low-tech translations system.

That low-tech approach was a purposeful strategy to inject ideas back into what felt like the overused void of media culture. For me, it was new technology that began to provide me with new content. And additional content, in my case, came from the new subject matter I was using. Pop and appropriation artists were using imagery that was already widely available. For me, there's a challenge and an amazing learning process in using new imaging and language systems as they're discovered.

If we're talking about the visual language of culture at a specific time, can you talk about the images and specialized visual vocabularies of the time that you wanted to explore?

My interest in the visual language of science and technology grew out of my growing disenchantment with painting. The habitual gestures of making paintings had become frustrating and were feeling meaningless. But because I like making paintings, I was caught in a contradiction. I was bored and frustrated, but I was still looking for new ways to bring some energy into the work. I started looking at Rorschach blots because they gave me a preexisting image to work with—somebody else's piece of paint, not my own. In the course of appropriating those forms, I inherited their content. Since I didn't want to paint Rorschach blots, I scanned images of them on a computer, made silk screens of them, and began to print them on canvas. By not being responsible for the image, by not being responsible for physically and traditionally painting an image, by having the meaning taken out of my hands, I found a perfect way to keep painting going for myself.

But, then, what was left for you to do?

What I started to appreciate was that inkblots tested for a kind of content I hadn't been thinking about when I started this work. I was using images from science that were used to test, on some level, someone else's psychic energy. Rorschach blots, from what I understand, while no longer used much, had once been thought useful in revealing pathology. Because the pathological aspects of culture fascinate me, I began to think about what else would constitute literal images of pathology. I started looking at medical textbooks, at images of viruses and cancers. I was interested in them both for what they were and what they looked like—completely abstract images as seen through an electron microscope. This was in 1987, when images like these weren't widely reproduced. Looking at them was like being under water in a coral sea, or being on the moon surrounded by lunar rocks. All of a sudden, I realized there was a whole other world that couldn't be seen by the eye but could be visualized through new technology. And the content of the images was really powerful, even if not very directly, at first, for a lay viewer.

> What interests me about images, all images, is that different communities make images for specific purposes and understand and use them differently, depending on their need, knowledge, and perspective. What was it like for you, a visual artist, to throw yourself into this new visual language of medical and scientific imagery?

The beauty of these images, to me, is they are the biological, technological, scientific equivalents of the Rorschach blots. I didn't know what these images meant; neither would anybody who wasn't a scientist. So, to answer your question, a scientist might look at an image and see technical information. ("This is the virus." "This is the cancer cell." "This is the healthy cell." "This is the cell in the bloodstream.") A contemporary art observer, looking at the same image, sees something perhaps closer to surrealism, a crazy juxtaposition of unknown things. What became interesting to me about the work was that, in an art context, images that were literal and useful to some became abstract and useful in another way to others. Unless I specifically name the images, you don't know what they are. So, viewers have the possibility of looking at paintings in a state of fantasy, of projecting onto them, or, at some point, going deeper and finding out what the images actually are of and about.

> How important is it, to you, that people know what they're looking at?

At one level, not important at all. I think art, especially painting, has to sustain viewing and work off of a certain level of visual interest. That has to do with aspects of surface, size, composition—all the technical, formal aspects of making a picture. Then, there's that other aspect of engagement, when an artwork starts making you ask questions. In the case of my work, it's logical to ask, "What is that? What am I looking at?" And if you do, that takes you to the next level of involvement. In the case of the work in this exhibition, if the wall label references my collaboration with Rod MacKinnon, who is a Nobel Prize winner in chemistry, that might lead you to ask some questions about painting or art history, about medicine and technology, or even, quite literally, about the meaning of life.

> *Let's talk about people's fascination with, and fear of, scientific images that seem to require a specialist's knowledge to understand.*

Since most people know little about molecular biology, this kind of specialized imagery can put viewers in a defensive position; it reminds them of how they struggled in high school math or chemistry. On the other hand, there are many ways to enter the work—other than dredging up memories of a set of equations on the chalkboard.

> *You talked earlier about your disenchantment with painting and about people's willingness to look at abstract images and test out something that's not clear to them. Photography seems to help ease that transition and helps make people feel grounded in what they're looking at. Photographic imagery plays a big role in your work; can you talk a bit about that?*

All of my work is photo-based. That's interesting to me because, while it's photo-based, you look at images that are microscopic, technical, and graspable, and yet there are no references in them to what looks like the real world. If you're sitting in front of the painting, in this exhibition, called *Potassium Channel* (pages 40–41), it looks pretty abstract. People have commented that it looks like "a landscape," an "aerial view," or "a satellite view of the world." In fact, the painting features a detail of the X-ray crystallography machines that Rod uses at Brookhaven National Laboratory to image his protein structure, so he can understand their function. The photograph, then, is both literal and abstract, and that's the part of photography that I love. What I also like about photography is that it's a quick way to get an image; one click and you've got it.

> *Yet, the work is far from what you'd characterize as photographic. You're painting and drawing on top of and around images all the time.*

... have given me an ... look at the non-equil behavior.

SS condition: $P_s \{ \alpha(H) + \alpha'(BH) \} = P_{SH} \{ \beta + \beta'(B) \}$ True for our measurements.

And $\frac{P_s}{P_{SH}}$ depends on B_{TOT} unless $\alpha \beta' k_B = \alpha' \beta$ (condition of microscopic reversibility). at -80 mV we see $\frac{\alpha' \beta}{\alpha \beta' k_B} = 3$. (ie. not equilib.)

Now we know that k_{on} ($= \alpha(H) + \alpha'(BH)$) is indep of volt and so α, α' are (most likely) indep of voltage. (V $\neq$ 0 is the only thing bringing our system out of equilib.) since at $v = 0$, $\alpha \beta' k_B = \alpha' \beta$ must hold, and since α, α' are indep of voltage, $\alpha k_B / \alpha'$ must be indep of volt. $\therefore \frac{\beta}{\beta'}$ at zero mV would be $= \alpha k_B / \alpha' \neq 0.002$. At -80 mV we have $\frac{\beta}{\beta'} = 0.006$.

(ie: $\frac{\alpha' \beta}{\alpha \beta' k_B} = 3 \rightarrow \frac{\alpha k_B}{\alpha'} = \frac{1}{3} \frac{\beta}{\beta'}$)

out ⌣ in

we have

$$\frac{\beta}{\beta'} = \frac{\beta_{out}(0) e^{\frac{\delta FV}{RT}} + \beta_{in}(0) e^{\frac{-\delta_2 FV}{RT}}}{\beta'}$$

Let's assume site nearer outside (ie sensitive only to outer pH and effect of mut on IV c/w this).

actually let's assume for moment symmetric pore: $\beta_{out}(0) = \beta_{in}(0)$ and $\delta_1 = \delta_2$.

$$\frac{\beta}{\beta'} = \frac{\beta(0)}{\beta'} \left[e^{\frac{\delta V}{25}} + e^{\frac{-\delta V}{25}} \right] = \frac{0.002}{\alpha k_B / \alpha'} \cosh\left(\frac{\delta V}{25}\right)$$

$v = 0 \Rightarrow \frac{\beta}{\beta'} = 0.002$

Let $\beta = \beta_{out} + \beta_{in}$
$\beta' \Rightarrow$ only to outside
Pretend volt - indep.

$\therefore \cosh\left(\frac{\delta(-80)}{25}\right) = 3 \rightarrow \delta = \frac{25}{80} \cosh^{-1}(3) = 0.55$ So that's interesting. $\delta \sim 0.5$.

note also? The result makes me wonder about diffusion with a lwd site in the middle. But realize that a symmetric pathway will give a special result — X, the thermodynamic driving force in $\frac{\pi_+}{\pi_-} = \bar{e}^{-X/kT}$ will be a perfectly even function of voltage.

$$S \underset{\beta + \beta'(B)}{\overset{\alpha(H) + \alpha'(BH)}{\rightleftharpoons}} SH$$

For steady state: $P_s \{ \alpha(H) + \alpha'(BH) \} = P_{SH} \{ \beta + \beta'(B) \}$ ie: Flux out must = Flux into a given state.

$\therefore \frac{P_s}{P_{SH}} = \frac{\beta + \beta'(B)}{\alpha(H) + \alpha'(BH)} \Big\} = const$ at steady state.

also

we also know for any path at equilib:

$P_s \alpha(H) = P_{SH} \beta \rightarrow \frac{P_s}{P_{SH}} = \frac{\beta}{\alpha(H)}$

and $P_s \alpha'(BH) = P_{SH} \beta'(B) \rightarrow \frac{P_s}{P_{SH}} = \frac{\beta'(B)}{\alpha'(BH)}$

$\therefore$ at equilib $\frac{\beta + \beta'(B)}{\alpha(H) + \alpha'(BH)} = \frac{\beta}{\alpha(H)} = \frac{\beta'(B)}{\alpha'(BH)}$

Note that is the case of detailed balance where the ratio of sums is indep of B_{TOT}.

I would say that ninety percent of my practice is drawing, which I love because I can work through ideas quickly. Painting is different, slower and more process-oriented. And, then, there's another visual language at work here—the texts and notations that come directly from Rod's notebooks, which I've photographed, and that introduce a whole other kind of mark-making and meaning.

Rod's texts suggest graffiti, which, historically, has played an interesting and sometimes controversial role in painting.

All that text is a record of touch; it's about human presence, which I like in the midst of all this technical imagery and information. The human touch and presence is important in this body of work; it reflects part of the process of a scientific discovery that's important because it helps explain how we function physiologically, biologically, and on a molecular level. The images and the text in this work are metaphors for the process of inquiry, of looking inside of the work we have to do.

Meaning?

Meaning, scientists are looking for something, looking for meaning, but so am I. So are you. So are most thinking people. We're all asking questions, trying to understand what forces make or shape who we are. Lots of people talk about that as being the job and a goal of both art and science.

Some people think the job of art is to be challenging. Others might want art to be pleasurable. No matter what your work may be about, no matter how scary the content may be, the work seems to strive toward a certain kind of beauty. How do you juggle the work's real-world content with the fact that you're making objects meant to be hung on walls and looked at?

Beauty is, for many, a forbidden word in art these days. I don't think that beauty is something you should strive for. I think it's the result of a process—how something is thought out, is constructed, and how it functions. If beauty is the by-product of a certain amount of experience, thinking, and collecting information that gets put on a canvas—and beauty is the result—then I'm all for it. But beauty is like a Rorschach blot, too. Someone might look at an image of a virus, for instance, and say, "Oh, my god, that's awful," and a scientist might look at that same image and say, "It's just incredible how the body works."

One of the things I like to talk about with both scientists and artists is their

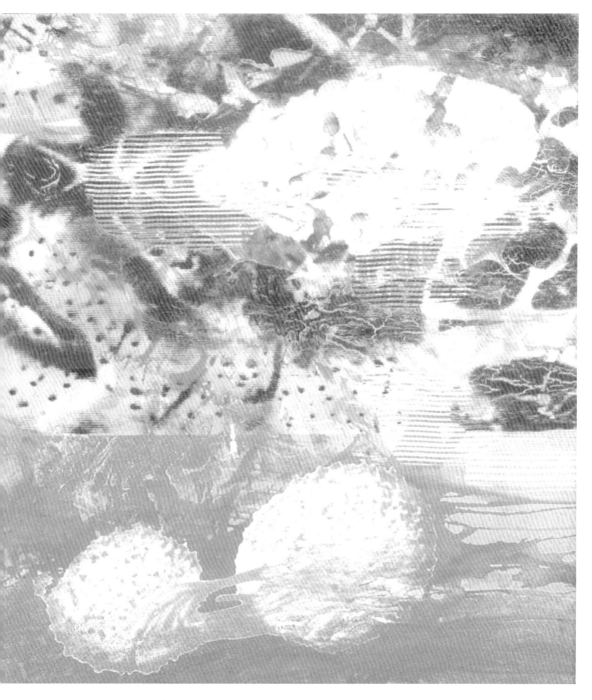

Sodium Glare 1989 (AIDS virus) 52x45" dispersion, silk screen on canvas

appreciation of, and fascination with, the process of searching and dealing with their work when things do or do not fall into place. You've spent a lot of time with scientists. What's similar about the ways artists and scientists work, about how they visualize and find their way through problems?

For painters, for instance, part of the beauty of a painting is knowing when to stop. There's a famous Monet quote: "The difference between me and any others is I know when to stop." If you overwork a painting, you kill it. With science, you keep going, no matter what. You keep exploring. And scientists keep looking, too, but the process is different; they work with very specific tools. The freedom in art is that you can let anything happen. When I talk to scientists, they never feel like they have that freedom to play. When I work with scientists and we start using the equipment, they always want to get everything in focus, to make everything work, to get me a certain kind of image. And I tend to say, "No. I want just the opposite of that. Do something you've never done before. Make it out of focus." They love to do that, but the equipment is so expensive and their tools are so rare, they feel they can't waste time and have to be efficient. The freedom of art is something scientists appreciate and, even, envy. One of the reasons I've been successful in working with scientists is because I give them the opportunity to play on someone else's dime.

A quality of the work in this exhibition that interests me is how, in the process of exploring the way that science is presented in imagery, there's a sense of spectacle and of the spectacular at work. The work is big. The images have an explosive quality about them. There's a sense of special effects at work. There's a sense of friction and excitement in the constant juxtaposition of language and image, the drawn versus the photographic. The work suggests that every body, every cell, literally and figuratively, is a spectacle, that something big is going on and needs to be looked at. And that something even bigger is yet to come.

I never thought about it that way until now, but the body is spectacular and the notion of spectacle is a big part of art and of culture. I've always been interested in work by artists like Jack Goldstein, who painted images of fireworks, volcanoes, and airplanes with contrails flying through the skies, dropping bombs. In work like that, there's a sense of watching a spectacle from a distance. In my work, the spectacle is just as big, but it takes place close by and on a much smaller and more intimate scale. What Rod MacKinnon does in his work is astounding. He figured out how a positively charged ion moves across a cell membrane, from a protein to a cell, at a rate of a hundred thousand to a million ions per second. That's a spectacle I never thought about as I was representing it, but when I step back and look at it, it is spectacular, on a macro-micro level. His work and the images it generates are cosmic in a sense; the ions he studies interconnect all of the electricity in the body so we can communicate with each other. Those are pretty incredible notions.

There's another level of spectacle at work, too: the massive amounts of money being spent on this research. Drug companies stand to make huge profits when they find the specific protein that targets a specific cell that's diseased. Which adds yet another level of complexity to the work: Science cures disease and makes money. The image of a virus or a protein that might kill or sidetrack disease looks beautiful in a painting. In that sense, the work mirrors the complexity of what's going on in the world today.

Since you've brought up macro-micro issues, let's end by addressing the issue of scale in this work.

Conventionally, scientists see their images reproduced small scale, in the lab or when they're published in journals. An image might get blown up in a PowerPoint presentation, but this kind of imagery is seldom seen on a large scale, or in a context removed from everyday work and the laboratory. When art and science intersect, it changes the context, beefs up the scale, and alters responses to imagery in unexpected ways. Images of the smallest of things become images you can get lost in. Scientists may not need or necessarily want that kind of scale or distraction. They're making science; they're looking for specific solutions. I'm making art and trying to communicate with a different audience, and scale is just one of the ways I try to do that.

What's ultimately important about all of this is that things and events minute in scale are monumental in terms of meaning and impact. Images are central to that process. Rod's work employs image-making for its function. Art is about function, too, but of a different kind. My job is to use specific kinds of images to grapple with the experiences of life and of culture, and to engage viewers in a dialogue about possibilities.

Marvin Heiferman, a curator and writer, has organized exhibitions and publications on art and visual culture for such institutions as the Museum of Modern Art, Smithsonian Institution, Whitney Museum of American Art, and International Museum of Photography.

1 Marshall McLuhan and Quentin Fiore, *War and Peace in the Global Village* (San Francisco: Hardwired, 1997), 12.

If They Exist 2007
80x85" dispersion, silk screen on canvas

above: **The Rug Under Which** 2007 81x59" dispersion, silk screen on canvas
right: **As We Understand More** 2007 80x60" dispersion, silk screen on canvas

At Any Given Moment 2007
80x60" dispersion and silk screen on canvas

above: **On the Outskirts** 2007 81x59" dispersion, silk screen on canvas
right: **The Chicken and the Egg Problem** 2007 80x60" dispersion and silk screen on canvas

above: **Potential Difference** 2007 81x49" dispersion and silk screen on canvas
right: **Increasingly Implausible** 2007 81x49" dispersion and silk screen on canvas

Definitely Tested 2007 80x80" dispersion and silk screen on canvas

Works in the Exhibition

Protein #203 2002 50x38" graphite, silk screen on paper, p. 25
Protein #220 2002 50x38" silk screen on paper, p. 42
Protein #236 2002 50x38" silk screen on paper, p. 30
Protein #299 2003 19x13" inkjet, pencil, silk screen on paper, p. 28
Protein #305 2003 19x13" inkjet, pencil, silk screen on paper, p. 26
Protein #321 2003 50x38" spray enamel, silk screen on paper, p. 24
Protein #356 2004 40x30" graphite, silk screen on paper, p. 23
Protein #364 2004 40x30" graphite, silk screen on paper, p. 22
Protein #375 2004 13x19" inkjet, graphite, silk screen on paper, p. 75
Protein #385 2004 50x38" graphite, silk screen on paper, p. 14
Protein #395 2004 19x13" pencil, enamel, silk screen on paper, p. 29
Protein #405 2005 19x13" graphite, silk screen on paper, p. 27
Fear of Flying 2003 46x36.5" dispersion, silk screen on canvas, p. 37
Signal Relay 2003 50x37.5" dispersion, silk screen on canvas, p. 47
Ongoing Advances 2003 75x51.5" dispersion and silk screen on canvas, p. 49
Super Symmetric 2004 25x19" dispersion, silk screen on canvas, p. 17
Soap Opera, the Second Season 2005 51x40" dispersion, silk screen on canvas, p. 12
Blackboard Jungle 2005 36x34" dispersion, silk screen on canvas, p. 19
    Collection Virginia Pierrepont
Silver Mine 2005 24x18" pencil, enamel, silk screen on canvas, p. 50
Liquid Wrap 2006 57x39.5" spray enamel, dispersion, silk screen on canvas, p. 15
Ice Queen 2006 24x18" pencil, dispersion, silk screen on canvas, p. 51
    Collection Johanne Miller
Crash 2006 26x20.5" dispersion, silk screen on canvas, p. 38
Hovercraft 2006 25x22" graphite, dispersion, silk screen on canvas, p. 11
    Collection Amy and Ronald Guttman
Illuminated Serum 2007 81x50.5" dispersion, silk screen on canvas, p. 13
Potassium Channel 2007 80.5"x81" dispersion, silk screen on canvas, pp. 40–41
Puppet State 2007 81x59.5" dispersion, silk screen on canvas, p. 16
We Need the Following Qualities 2007 38.5x29" dispersion, silk screen on canvas, p. 44
Thought Balloon 2007 25x20.5" dispersion, silk screen on canvas, p. 45
Crystal Clear 2007 38.5x28" dispersion, silk screen on canvas, p. 35
Potential Difference 2007 81x49" dispersion, silk screen on canvas, p. 70
If They Exist 2007 80x85" dispersion, silk screen on canvas, pp. 62–63
As We Understand More 2007 80x60" dispersion, silk screen on canvas, p. 65
    Collection Lisa Phillips
Increasingly Implausible 2007 81x49" dispersion, silk screen on canvas, p. 71
The Chicken and the Egg Problem 2007 80x60" dispersion, silk screen on canvas, p. 69
Definitely Tested 2007 80x80" dispersion, silk screen on canvas, pp. 72–73
At Any Given Moment 2007 81x88" dispersion, silk screen on canvas, pp. 66–67
    Collection Beth Rudin DeWoody
The Rug Under Which 2007 81x59" dispersion, silk screen on canvas, p. 64
On the Outskirts 2007 81x59" dispersion, silk screen on canvas, p. 68

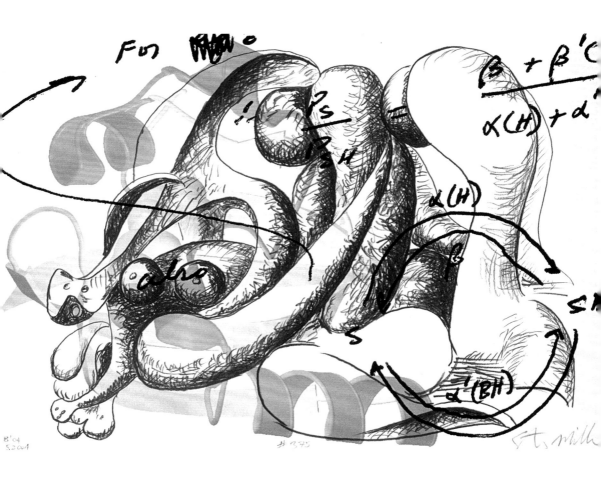

Protein #375 2004 13x19" inkjet, graphite, silk screen on paper

Solo Exhibitions

2007 The Rose Art Museum, Brandeis University, Waltham, Massachusetts
2003 Galerie Lilian Andree, Basel, Switzerland
2002 Raphael Rigassi Gallery, Bern, Switzerland
        Universal Concepts Unlimited, New York
2000 "Neomort," Universal Concepts Unlimited, New York
1999 Hong Kong Arts Center, China
1998 Karin Sachs Gallery, Munich, Germany
1996 Centre International d'Art Visuels–Cargo, Marseilles, France
        Espace d'Art Yvonamor Palix, Paris, France
        CAPC Musée Bordeaux, France
1994 Espace d'Art Brenne, France
1993 Karin Sachs Gallery, Munich, Germany
        Nina Freudenheim Gallery, Buffalo, New York
        A. B. Galeries, Paris, France
1992 Elga Wimmer Gallery, New York
1991 Galerie du Genie, Paris, France
1989 Fiction/non fiction, New York
        Carol Getz Gallery, Miami, Florida
        Galerie du Genie, Paris, France
1987 Josh Baer Gallery, New York
1986 Jack Shainman Gallery, Washington, D.C.
        Josh Baer Gallery, New York
1985 Public Art Fund—Times Square Electronic Billboard, New York
        Jack Shainman Gallery, Washington, D.C.
        Bette Stoler Gallery, New York
1982 Artists Space, New York
1981 White Columns, New York

Selected Group Exhibitions

2007 "Brasil Des Focus: o olho de fora," curated by Paulo Herkenhoff and Nessia Leonzini, Centro Cultural Banco do Brasil, Rio de Janeiro, Brazil
2006 "Neuroculture: Visual Art and the Brain," curated by Suzanne Anker and Giovanni Frazzetto, Westport Art Center, Westport, Connecticut
2005 "Finders Keepers," curated by Alicia Longwell, Parrish Art Museum, Southampton, New York
        "Abstraction," Burchfield-Penney Art Center, Buffalo, New York
        "Edge of Nature," Jameson Ellis and Steve Miller, curated by Graham Leader, Hampton Road Gallery, Southampton, New York
        "Le Cas du Sac," Musée de la Mode et du Textile, Paris, France
        "Collection 2," Fondation pour l'Art Contemporain Claudine et Jean-Marc Salomon, Annency, France
        "Colecoes IV," curated by Nessia Leonzini, Mercedes Viegas Arte Contemporanea, Rio de Janeiro, Brazil
        "Reprotech: Building Better Babies," curated by Suzanne Anker, The New York Academy of Sciences, New York
        "Touch and Temperature: Art in the Age of Cybernetic Totalism," curated by Michael Rees, Bitforms Gallery, New York
2003 "Divining Fragments: Reconciling the Body," curated by Koan-Jeff Baysa, The Center for Photography at Woodstock, New York
        "From Code to Commodity: Genetics and Visual Art," curated by Suzanne Anker, The New York Academy of Sciences, New York
        "Genomic Issue(s): Art and Science," curated by Marvin Heiferman and Karin Sinsheimer, The Graduate Center of the City University of New York, New York
2001 "Digital Printmaking Now," curated by Marylin Kushner, Brooklyn Museum of Art, New York
2000 "Paradise Now: Creating the Genetic Revolution," curated by Marvin Heiferman and Carol Kismaric, Exit Art, New York
        "Cyberarts 2000," Prix Ars Electronica, Linz, Austria
1999 "Dreams 1900–2000," curated by Lynn Gamwell, Equitable Art Gallery, New York

1998 "Autour du Mondial," Galerie Enrico Navarra, Paris, France
1997 "Sous le Manteau," Galerie Thaddaeus Ropac, Paris, France
1996 "Steve Miller & Joseph Nechvatal," Parsons Gallery, Paris, France
1995 "Morceau Choisis, du Fonds National d'Art Contemporain," Centre National d'Art
Contemporain de Grenoble, France
"Imaging the Body, an Artistic Diagnosis," The New York Academy of Sciences, New York
"Autour de Roger Vivier," Galerie Enrico Navarra, Paris, France
"In Corpus Machina—Keith Cottingham, Steve Miller, Joseph Nechvatal," Espace d'Art,
Yvonamor Palix, Paris, France
"Humanism and Technology: The Human Figure in Industrial Society," curated by Pierre
Restany, National Museum of Contemporary Art, Seoul, Korea
"The Outside Inside Gertrude Stein," Dortmunder Kunstverein, Dortmund, Germany
1994 "Gene Culture," curated by Suzanne Anker, Fordham College, New York
"Logo non Logo," curated by Robert Morgan and Pierre Restany, Thread Waxing Space, New
York
1993 "Compkuenstlerg," Kunstlerwerkstatt Lothringer Strasse, Munich, Germany
"The Return of the Cadavre Exquis," The Drawing Center, New York
1992 "Excess in the Techno-Mediacratic Society," curated by Joseph Nechvatal, Musée Sarret de
Grozon, Arbois, France
1991 "Byron, French, Miller, Solomoukha," Elga Wimmer Gallery, New York
"Art, Science et Materiaux," L'Institut des Materiaux, Nantes, France
1990 "V.I.P.-Video-Image(s)-Peinture," Galerie du Genie, Paris, France
"Not Painting: Goldstein, Miller, Paik, Richter," S. Bitter-Larkin Gallery, New York
"Komoski, Miller, Minter," Carol Getz Gallery, Miami, Florida
1989 "Chaos," curated by Laura Trippi, The New Museum of Art, New York
"Science/Technology/Abstraction," curated by Barry A. Rosenberg, Wright State University,
Dayton, Ohio
1987 "Computer Assisted: The Computer in Contemporary Art," Freedman Gallery, Albright College,
Reading, Pennsylvania
"Computers and Art," Contemporary Arts Center, Cincinnati, Ohio
"Dwyer, Jackson, Miller," Nina Freudenheim, Buffalo, New York
"Digital Visions: Computers and Art," curated by Cynthia Goodman, Everson Museum of Art,
Syracuse, New York
"The 2nd Emerging Expressions Biennial: The Artist and the Computer," Bronx Museum of the
Arts, New York
"New York: New Venue," curated by Lisa Phillips, The Mint Museum, Charlotte, North Carolina
1986 "Physics," Colin De Land Fine Art, New York
"Dwyer, Lemieux, Majore, Miller, Nagy, Tim Rollins & KOS," Rhona Hoffman, Chicago, Illinois
"Brown, Miller, Nagy, Suzuki," Colin De Land Fine Art, New York
1985 "Dwyer, Spero, Majore, Miller, Lang," Josh Baer Gallery, New York
"Emerging Expressions: The Artist and the Computer," Bronx Museum of the Arts, New York
"Past & Future Perfect," Hallwalls, Buffalo, New York
1984 "Bialobroda, Blair, Miller, Rosenberg," Baskerville & Watson Gallery, New York
"Between Here & Nowhere," curated by Rosetta Brooks Riverside Studios, London
"Group Show," International with Monument, New York
"Behind Faces & Figures," Philadelphia College of Art, Philadelphia, Pennsylvania
1983 "Language, Drama, Source & Vision," curated by Lynn Gumpert, Ned Rifkin, and Marcia
Tucker, The New Museum, New York
"Steve Miller & Brigid Kennedy," Burchfield Center, Buffalo, New York
"Shared Space," curated by Phillip Verre, Bronx Museum of the Arts, New York
1982 "The Ritz Hotel," Washington Project for the Arts, Washington, D.C.
"Visual Politics," Alternative Museum, New York
"New Drawing in America," The Drawing Center, New York
"The Crime Show," ABC NO RIO, New York
1981 "Selections Sixteen," The Drawing Center, New York
1979 "Six Artists Under Thirty," curated by Edna Lindeman, Burchfield Center, Buffalo, New York
"Dimensions Variable," curated by Susan Logan, Allan Schwartzman, and Kathleen Thomas,
The New Museum, New York
1978 "Contemporary Reflections," Aldrich Museum, Ridgefield, Connecticut

Bibliography

Rogers, Pat. *The Southampton Press* (July 19, 2007): "Pottery Tells of Chinese History."

de Malherbe, Delphine. *Icono Fly* (Sommaire No. 2, 2007): Editorial, "Journal D'une Montre."

de Malherbe, Delphine. *Icono Fly* (Sommaire No. 1, 2006): Editorial, "Le Sac de Voyage."

Rogers, Pat. *The Southampton Press* (December 22 & 29, 2005): "Finding Link Between Art and Science, Ancient Objects Are Inspiration for Artist."

Landes, Jennifer. *The East Hampton Star* (December 15, 2005): "Obsessions on Display."

Ernst, Eric. *The Southampton Press* (November 24, 2005): "Is Collecting Also Creating? Parrish Show Finds Works on eBay, Not at Sotheby's."

Anker, Suzanne. *Update: New York Academy of Sciences Magazine* (April/May 2004): "Reprotech: Building Better Babies."

Baysa, Kóan-Jeff. *NY Arts* (December 2003): "Divining Fragments: Reconciling the Body."

Anker, Suzanne. *Leonardo* (Vol. 33, No. 5, 2000): "Gene Culture: Molecular Metaphor in Visual Art."

Travis, John. *Science News* (Vol. 158, No. 25, December 16, 2000): "Genes on Display: DNA Becomes Part of the Artist's Palette."

Schjeldahl, Peter. *The New Yorker* (October 2, 2000): "DNART, a Show Embraces Biomania."

Laber, Emily. *The Sciences* (September/October 2000): "Variations on a Gene."

Rush, Michael. *Art in America* (July 2000): "Steve Miller at Universal Concepts Unlimited."

Katz, Carissa. *The East Hampton Star* (September 23, 1999): "Steve Miller: Seeing through His Subjects."

Artslink, Hong Kong Arts Center Magazine (March 1999): "Self-Portrait Vanitas: Steve Miller."

Au, Desirée. *South China Morning Post* (March 12, 1999): "Artist's Brush with Technology."

Einzig, Barbara. *Artbyte* (Vol. 1, No. 6, February/March 1999): "Steve Miller/Accessory Access."

Paris Review (No. 147, Summer 1998): front cover, "Self-Portrait Vanitas #55," 1998.

Wiedemann, Christophe. *Suddeutsche Zeitung* (March 12, 1998): "Computer Art: New Impressions of Skulls and Flowers, Steve Miller at Karin Sachs Gallery."

Kunzru, Hari. *Wired* (June l996): "Art and Invention."

L'Officiel (No. 804, April 1996): "Echographies Affectives."

Berthemy, Odile. *Angeline's* (No. 8, spring 1996): "Steve Miller ou "l'Espace du Dedans."

Miller, Steve. *Leonardo* (Vol. 29, No. 1, February 1996): "Portrait of Isabel Goldsmith."

Mattieussent, Brice. *Expositions: Pour Walter Benjamin* (Fourbis, Paris, 1994): "Les 'psychicones' de Steve Miller."

Morice, Anne-Marie. *La Croix L'Evenement* (August 13, 1994): "Steve Miller au Pays de Brenne."

Huser, France. *Le Nouvel Observateur* (July 28–August 3, 1994): "L'Art et la Science."

La Nouvelle Republique (June 25–26, 1994): "L'Origine du Monde Selon Miller."

Matthieussent, Brice. *art press* (No. 187, January 1994): "Steve Miller: A. B. Galeries."

Beaux Arts Magazine (No. 118, December 1993): "Steve Miller: Le Virus de L'Image."

Breerette, Genevieve. *Le Monde* (November 11, 1993): "Steve Miller at A. B. Galerie."

Chevaleyre, Patrick. *Le Journal des Expositions* (October 1993): "Steve Miller."

Huntington, Richard. *The Buffalo News* (October 14, 1993): "Self-Portraits from the Inside Out."

Pagel, David. *Los Angeles Times* (August 7, 1993): "Techno Domination."

Suddeutsche Zeitung (March 23, 1993): Karin Sachs Solo Exhibition.

Gerit, Henry. *Art News* (October 1992): "Steve Miller at Elga Wimmer."

Hagen, Charles. *The New York Times* (June 12, 1992): "Art in Review—'Technological Alienation.'"

art press special (October 1991): "Steve Miller—Vers Une Peinture Virtuelle."

Bataillon, Francoise. *Beaux Arts Magazine* (February 1991, No. 87): "Expose—Steve Miller/Pixels Contre Peinture."

Mahoney, Robert. *Galeries Magazine* (February/March 1991): "Steve Miller—A New Disease in Painting."

Mahoney, Robert. *Contemporane* (No. 24, January 1991): "V.I.P. (Video—Images—Painting)."

Sarrazin, Stephen. *art press* (No. 153, December 1990): "Video—Images—Peinture."

Grundberg, Andy. *The New York Times* (April 27, 1990): "Photography Review—'Not Painting.'"

Turner, Elisa. *The Miami Herald* (April 4, 1990): "Three New York Artists Play with Perception."

Cone, Michele. *art press* (No. 141, November 1989): "Strange Attractors/Signs of Chaos."

Print Collector's Newsletter (November–December 1989): "Prints and Photographs Published/Steve Miller."

Turner, Elisa. *The Miami Herald* (April 12, 1989): "Complex Works Stretch Limits of Graffiti Art."

Zanzotto, Andrea. *art press* (No. 130, November 1988): "Polemiques a New York: Hier et Aujourd'hui."

Smulders, Caroline. *OPUS International* (November–December 1988): "Steve Miller/Galerie du Genie."

Le Monde (October 5, 1988): "Une Nuit à la Bastille."

Huntington, Richard. *Buffalo News* (September 27, 1988): "Twenty in New York."

McCormick, Carlo. *Artforum* (May 1988): "Steve Miller/Josh Baer Gallery."

Hagen, Charles. *ZG* (April 1988): "Altered States."

Haus, Mary-Ellen. *Art News* (April 1988): "Steve Miller at Josh Baer."

Levin, Kim. *Village Voice* (February 2, 1988): "Voice Choices/Art."

Huntington, Richard. *Buffalo News* (September 18, 1987): "Varied Works Make Appealing Mix in Freudenheim Exhibition."

McCormick, Carlo. *High Times* (No. 132, August 1986): "Neo-Psychedelia: An Art Exhibit for the 80s."

Cameron, Dan. *Arts Magazine* (summer 1986): "Report from the Front."

Jones, Ronald. *Flash Art* (No. 128, May–June 1986): "Steve Miller at Josh Baer."

Decter, Joshua. *Arts Magazine* (May 1986): "Steve Miller at Josh Baer."

Bannon, Anthony. *Buffalo News* (April 10, 1985): "Exhibit Looks to Past, Illuminates the Future."

Baer, Josh. *ZG* (No. 13, spring 1985): "Twilight Zone 1985."

Coleman, Nicols. *The Washington Post* (April 11, 1985): "Paintings by Steve Miller."

Bannon, Anthony. *Buffalo News* (March 10, 1985): "Recent Gallery Acquisitions Put Sculpture on a Pedestal."

Brooks, Rosetta. *Artforum* (February 1985): "From the Night of Consumerism to the Dawn of Simulation."

Hatton, Brian. *Flash Art* (January 1985): "Between Here & Nowhere."

Gooding, Mel. *Artscribe* (No. 49, November–December 1984): "Ronald Reagan's Charm—Rosetta Brooks Interviewed by Mel Gooding."

Shepard, Joan. *New York Daily News* (January 20, 1984): "Art Meets the Machine, Again."

Wolff, Theodore F. *The Christian Science Monitor* (October 31, 1983): "A Place for Today's Most Challenging Art."

Bannon, Anthony. *Buffalo News* (June 3, 1983): "Area Natives Shine in 3 Exhibitions."

Zimmer, William. *The New York Times* (May 15, 1983): "A Kind of Harmony at the Bronx Museum."

Glueck, Grace. *The New York Times* (May 13, 1983): "Three Shows Open New Bronx Museum."

Cavaliere, Barbara. *Arts Magazine* (February 1982): "Steve Miller at White Columns."

Zimmer, William. *Soho Weekly News* (December 1, 1981): "Selections 16."

Zimmer, William. *Soho Weekly News* (June 25, 1980): "Art Pick."

Zimmer, William. *Soho Weekly News* (October 1, 1979): "Ocular Mechanics."

Larson, Kay. *Village Voice* (October 22, 1979): "Dimensions Variable."

Catalogues and Books

2007 *Brasil Des Focos (o olho de fora),* Nessia Leonzini and Paulo Herkenhoff, Centro Cultural Banco do Brasil, Rio de Janeiro, Brazil.
From Technological to Virtual Art, Frank Popper Leonardo Books, MIT Press.

2006 *Eat Protein*, Steve Miller, artist's book, edition of 16 examples.
Neuroculture, Visual Art and the Brain, Suzanne Anker and Giovanni Frazzetto, Westport Art Center, Westport, Connecticut.

2005 *Kunst Aus Dem Labor:* Zum Verhältnis von Kunst und Wissenschaft im Zeitalter der Technoscience, Ingeborg Reichle, Edition Springer Wien New York, Vienna, Austria.
Collection 2, Phillippe Piquet, La Fondation pour l'Art Contemporain, Claudine et Jean-Marc Salomon, Annency, France.

2004 *Photographie Plasticienne, L'Extreme Contemporain*, Dominique Baque, Editions du Regard, Paris, France.
Carried Away, All About Bags, general editor: Farid Chenoune, Union Central des Arts décoratifs, Le Passage Paris—New York Editions.

2003 *The Molecular Gaze, Art in the Genetic Age*, Suzanne Anker and Dorothy Nelkin, Cold Spring Harbor Laboratory Press.
Genomic Issue(s): Art & Science, Marvin Heiferman and Karen Sinsheimer Art Gallery of the Graduate Center, New York.
From Code to Commodity: Genetics and Visual Art, Dorothy Nelkin and Suzanne Anker, New York Academy of Sciences

2002 *Information Arts: Intersections of Art, Science, and Technology*, Stephen Wilson, Leonardo Books, MIT Press.

2001 *Notes for Neolithic Quark,* Universal Concepts Unlimited, New York.
  Digital Printmaking Now, Marylin Kushner, Brooklyn Museum of Art, New York.
  Mondial, Enrico Navarra, Paris, France.
2000 *Paradise Now, Picturing the Genetic Revolution*, Marvin Heiferman and Carol Kismaric, Tang Art Museum, Saratoga Springs, New York.
  13 Alumni Artists, edited by Emmie Donadio, essay by Lisa Phillips and Avital Ronell, Middlebury College Museum of Art, Middlebury, Vermont.
  Dreams 1900–2000, Science Art and the Unconscious Mind, Lynn Gamwell, Cornell University Press.
1998 *80 Artistes Autour du Mondial*, Nicolas Bourriaud, Giles de Bure, Henri-Francois Debailleux, Paul Lombard, Michel Nuridsany, Pierre Restany, Galerie Enrico Navarra, Paris, France.
  Bettyann Holtzman Kevles, *Naked to the Bone*, Rutgers University Press.
1997 *Sous le Manteau,* Caroline Smulders, Galerie Thaddaeus Ropac, Paris, France.
1995 *Morceaux Choisis,* du Fonds National d'Art Contemporain, Centre National d'Art Contemporain de Grenoble, France.
  Autour de Roger Vivier, Enrico Navarra Gallery, Paris, France.
  The Outside Inside Gertrude Stein, Ina Ewers-Schultz, Dortmunder Kunstverein, Germany.
  Gene Culture: Molecular Metaphore in Visual Art, Suzanne Anker, Fordham College, New York.
  Humanism and Technology, The Human Figure in Industrial Society, Pierre Restany, National Museum of Contemporary Art, Seoul, Korea .
1994 *Logo non Logo*, Robert C. Morgan and Pierre Restany, Thread Waxing Space, New York.
  Steve Miller: l'Origine du Monde, Brice Matthieussent, Espace Art Brenne, France.
  Les Americains, Alain Tourneaux, Palais Benedictine, Fecamp, France.
1993 *Computerunterstutzte Kunst,* Christoph Wiedmann, Kunstlerwerkstatt Lothringerstrasse, Munich, Germany.
  Steve Miller, Simon Lane, A. B. Galeries, Paris, France.
1992 *Steve Miller*, Dan Cameron, Elga Wimmer Gallery New York.
  Excess in the Techno Mediacratic Society, Joseph Nechvatal, Didier Gagneur, Toby Crokett, and Robert C. Morgan, Musée Sarret de Grozon, Arbois, France.
1991 *Steve Miller*, David Corey, Galerie du Genie, Paris, France.
1990 *V.I.P.—video—image—peinture*, Stephen Sarrazin and Don Foresta, Galerie du Genie, Paris, France.
  Not Painting: Jack Goldstein, Steve Miller, Nam June Paik, Gerhard Richter, Robert Mahoney, S. Bitter-Larkin Gallery, Nadelstein Press, New York.
1989 *Strange Attractors Signs Of Chaos*, Laura Trippi, The New Museum of Contemporary Art, New York.
  Science/Technology/Abstraction, Barry A. Rosenberg, University Art Galleries, Wright State University, Dayton, Ohio.
1988 *Steve Miller*, Galerie du Genie, Paris, France.
1987 *Beyond Boundaries—New York's New Art*, Jerry Saltz, Alfred Van Der Marck Editions
  New York, New Venue, Lisa Phillips, The Mint Museum, Charlotte, North Carolina.
  Digital Visions, Cynthia Goodman, Harry N. Abrams, New York.
  The Second Emerging Expressions Biennial: The Artist and the Computer, Patric Prince, Shalom Gorewitz, Bronx Museum of Art, New York.
  Computer Assisted: The Computer in Contemporary Art, David S. Rubin, Freedman Gallery, Albright College, Reading, Pennsylvania.
1984 *Between Here & Nowhere*, Rosetta Brooks, Riverside Studios, London, United Kingdom.
1983 *Steve Miller: Five New Works*, Rosetta Brooks, Burchfield Center, Buffalo, New York.
  Shared Space, Phillip Verre, Bronx Museum, Bronx, New York.
1982 *New Drawing in America*, Martha Beck and Marie Keller, The Drawing Center, New York.
1979 *Dimensions Variable,* Susan Logan, Allan Schwartzman and Kathleen Thomas, The New Museum, New York.
  Six Artists under Thirty, Edna Lindeman, Burchfield Center, Buffalo, New York.

Steve Miller would like to thank his collaborators Lori Loper, Becky Rosko, Henry Sanchez, and John Wilton for their creative energy in making the work for this exhibition.

*right: **Rod MacKinnon and Steve Miller***